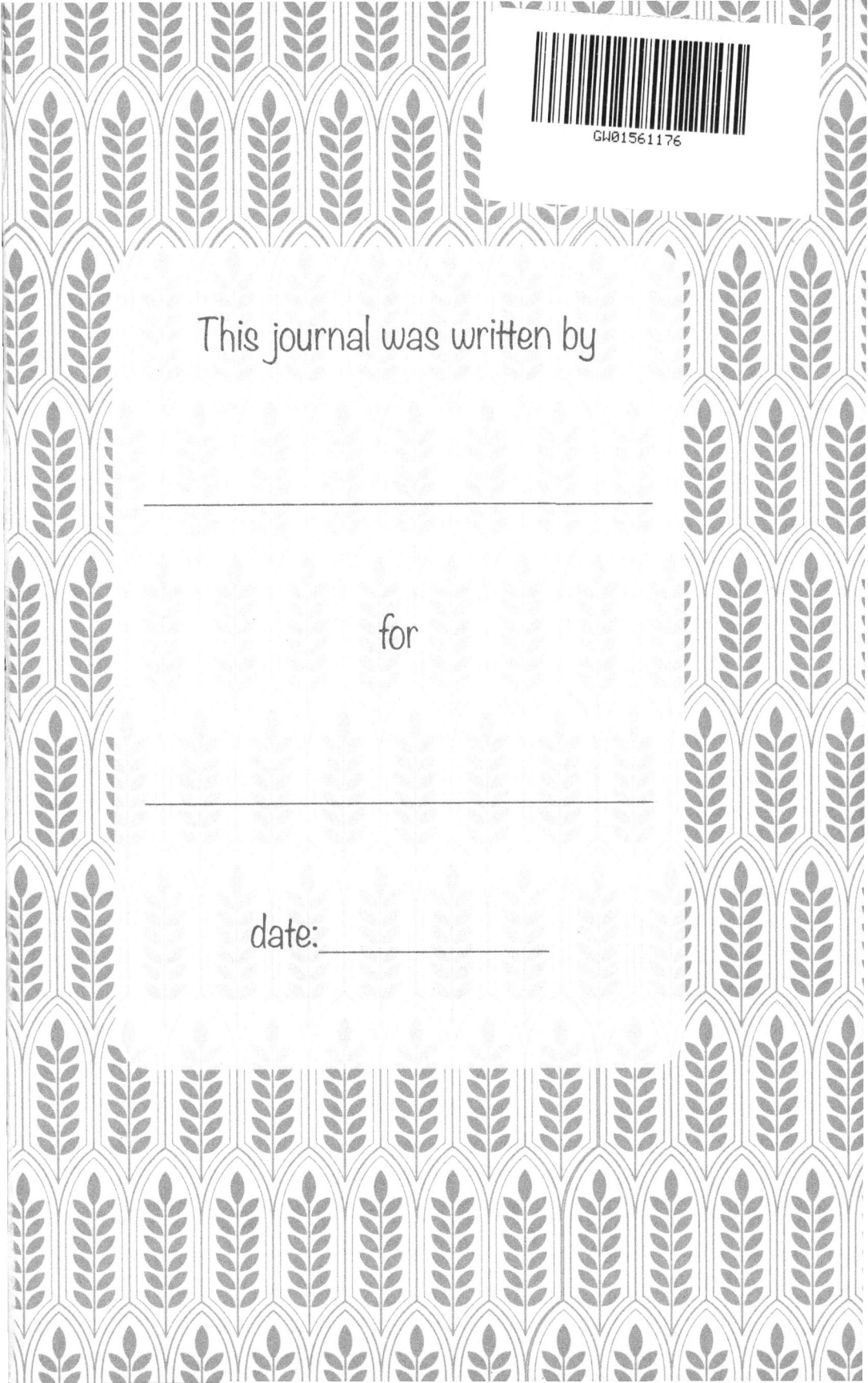

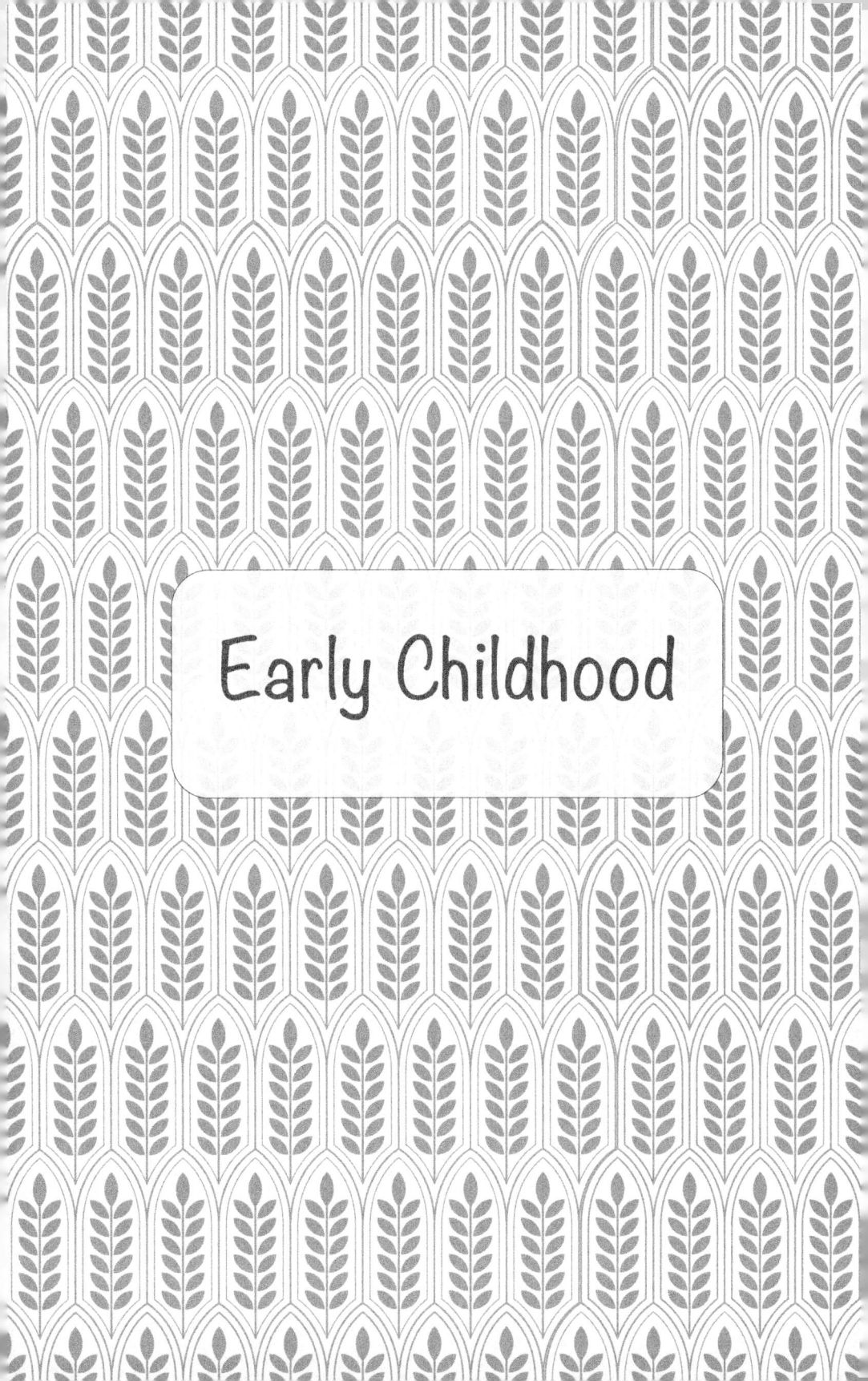
Early Childhood

When and where were you born?
Were you born in a hospital, at home or elsewhere?

What is your full name that you were born with.. How did your parents choose your name, and does it have a special meaning?

What are the names of your parents and siblings?

Did you have any nicknames?

When and where were your family members born? What countries do our people come from?

What kinds of things did your family do together when you were young?

How did you celebrate special times like Christmas and birthdays?

What were your favorite toys as a child? What games did you play?

What kind of books did you like to read?

What are the earliest memories about your first home?
What about other homes and places you lived?

Who were some of your friends, and what are your fondest memories of spending time with them?

What schools did you attend?

What were your favorite subjects in school?

Who were your favorite teachers and why were they your favorite?

Did you have any childhood diseases?

Did you ever do anything naughty/mischievous?

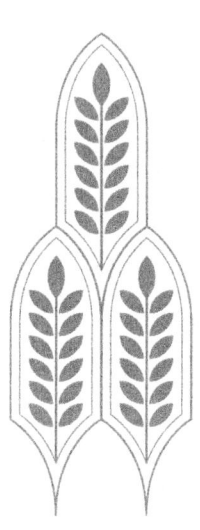

Later Childhood

What did you do when you were a teenager?

Did you and your friends have a special place to hangout?

What has defined you?

What were your happiest moments?

Write about your parents, grandparents, and siblings.

What were the occupations of your parents?

What do you remember most about your mother?

What do you remember most about your father?

What do you remember most about your grandparents?

Did you ever have a pet?

What were your goals for the future?

Where have you lived?

What experiences in your life have molded you into the person you are today?

How has the world changed?

Who are/were your best friends?

What's the one thing you would do differently?

What do you remember most about your childhood?

What family trip do you remember most?

Write a letter to your teenage self:-

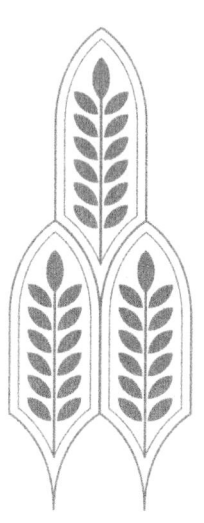

Early Adulthood

Who have you worked for, and what jobs did you do?

What has your work life been like?

How many times have you been in love?

Who was your first date?

Do you remember your first kiss?

What do you want your great- and great-great-grandchildren to know about you?

What role has money played in your life?

Have you experienced hardship?

What was your favorite vacation?

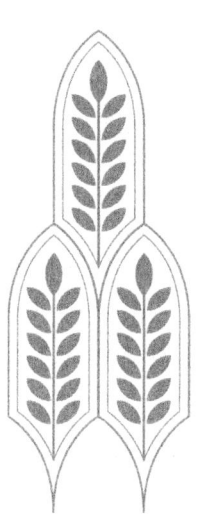

Starting a Family

How did you meet the love of your life?

What was your proposal like?

Where was your wedding? How many people attended? What was the ceremony like?

Did you have a honeymoon? Where did you go?

How many children did you have all together?
What are their names, birthdates and birthplaces?

Why did you name them what you did?

Are there any funny or unusual things your children did that stand out?

What was most rewarding about being a parent?

Were you strict or lenient as a parent?

What are some special memories you have about your children?

Write a letter to yourself as a new father

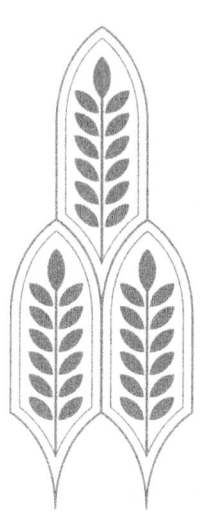

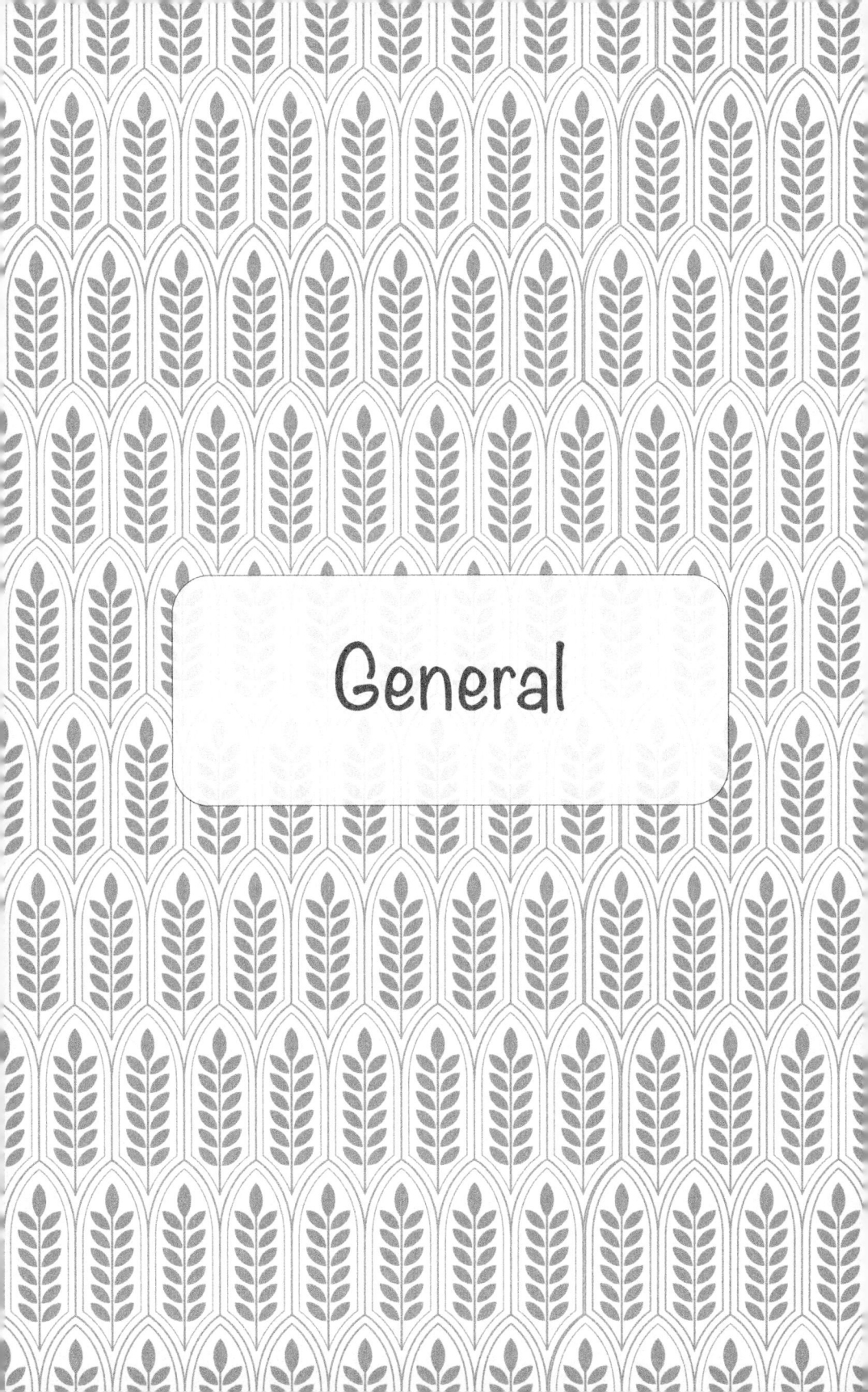

What are your favorite things to do now?

What do you hope for your children and grandchildren?

Do you remember your grandparents describing their lives? What did they say?

When and where did your parents die? What do you remember about that? How did they die?

Have you ever been the victim of a crime?

Have you been in a serious accident?

Has anyone ever saved your life?

What is the funniest family story you remember?

What is your favorite book, movie and song?

What do you think are the great inventions in your lifetime?

Do you remember the first time you saw a computer or a mobile phone?

Do you remember your family discussing world events and politics?

How would you describe yourself politically?

What is your medical and genetic history?

What traditions do you most want our family to continue?

Are there any old family secrets you can now share?

What is the bravest thing you have ever done?

Who is the person you would most like to meet?

How have you changed over the last 10 years?

What is your most treasured possession?

What was the most fun you ever had?

If a genie granted you 3 wishes - what would they be?

If you could be an expert in anything - what would it be?

What was your proudest moment?

What are your favorite meals and desserts?

What always brings tears to your eyes?

What DIY tips and general home maintenance advice do you want to pass on?

Printed in Great Britain
by Amazon